you often say, "I would give, but only
to the deserving."
The trees in your orchard say
not so, nor the flocks in your
pasture.
They give that they may live,
for to withhold is to perish.
See first that you yourself
deserve to be a giver, and an
instrument of giving.
For in truth it is life that gives
unto life — while you, who
deem yourself a giver, are
but a witness.

12/12/80

your friend —
Virginia Atter Keys

WJAX

Florida Sketches

Hampton Dunn

Florida Sketches

a delightful tour in text
and pictures of some of the most
fascinating sights and landmarks
of Florida

 E. A. Seemann Publishing, Inc.
Miami, Florida

To

Mrs. HARRIET HOLT CONNELL

my English teacher at Citrus High School who, bless her,
tried her darnedest to teach me good grammar and a bit
about writing.

Contents

Florida Sketches

PIONEER DOCTOR AND BOTANIST

APALACHICOLA–"He loved every living and growing thing and welcomed each season as 'the book of nature turned its leaves.' "

This description is of Dr. Alvah Wentworth Chapman, a physician in pioneer North Florida, who took up botany as a hobby and wrote a *Flora of the Southern United States* which remains a standard work in the field today.

The weather-beaten house where Dr. Chapman lived and served his fellow man is located on the main street of Apalachicola and is a boarding house today, the White House Hotel. It is one of only three mansions surviving from the days when Apalachicola was a thriving port city.

A native of Massachusetts, Dr. Chapman at one time taught school in Georgia and came to Florida in 1835, first to Quincy, then to Marianna, and finally to Apalachicola in 1847 where he died in 1899. His busy life included service as County Judge, Mayor, Collector of Customs (from 1866 to 1870, when the revenues of the city were the largest it ever had).

Dr. Chapman narrowly escaped capture by the Indians near Saint Marks where he was looking for a native tree, titi. In a letter from Quincy he wrote in 1840: "I am on the frontier and the Indians hold undisturbed possession of the country between me and the Gulf . . ." a genus of plants, known as Chapmania, commemorates his name.

The Botanical Gazette said of the Floridian: "With his demise passed away the Nestor of American botanists; the last of the great workers to whom the great progress made in the past 60 years on the exploration and investigation of the flora of this continent is to be ascribed."

THE MAMMOTH IN FLORIDA

BARTOW—If you're crusing along State Road 60 east of Bartow and you see an oversize "elephant" poised along the highway, don't be startled. What you are seeing is a statue of a Pleistocene mammoth, one of the giant animals which roamed the Florida peninsula in prehistoric times. The statue is a trademark for the Phosphate Valley Exposition on this site. The North American Imperial Mammoth attained a shoulder height of fourteen feet.

This area is the heart of the state's phosphate-producing industry, where eighty percent of the nation's phosphate is mined. Scooped up often in this activity are the fossilized bones of mastodons, saber-toothed tigers, and blue triangles with serrated edges, the teeth of big sharks which once swam the warm shallow seas covering the state eons ago. The local museum shows a splendid collection of pleistocene fossils, said to be far more complete than that of the Smithsonian Institution.

Shortly after the phosphate boom began in Florida, the *Florida Times-Union* of Jacksonville reported that phosphate beds were "the petrified remains of countless millions of animals whose existence dates back into the gray dawn of time . . . but in carrying out God's plan, these huge monsters . . . buried through all these millions of forgotten ages, again come forth in other forms to give luxuriance and fertility to the plant life which feeds a hungry people, proving that 'Life is constantly nursing at the bosom of death.' "

A LEGEND IN ITS TIME

BOCA RATON—Few resorts in the United States, perhaps in all the world, are so richly endowed with a flamboyant past equal to that of the incomparable Boca Raton Hotel & Club.

The resort was designed as a hotel by Addison Mizner who was more widely remembered as a wit and dilettante than as a superb artist and maybe a genius. Someone even called him "the poet of architects."

The Boca Raton Hotel & Club, first called the Cloister Inn, was one of Mizner's greatest creations. The 100-room inn was built at a cost of $1.2 million, and the designer had a field day treating the Spanish-Gothic architecture in the Mizner manner.

The elegant inn was in keeping with the carefree, happy days of the 1920s, and opening night on February 6, 1926, at the height of the Florida real estate boom, saw royalty, film stars, and the world's wealthiest people arrive in their most luxurious cars—Duesenbergs, Pierce Arrows, Packards, and Cadillacs. Some of the big names who dined that night in the gracious Cathedral Dining Room were former heavyweight champion John L. Sullivan, film stars Marie Dressler and Al Jolson, Mrs. Vincent Astor, Irene Castle McLaughlin, Countess Salm, Myron Taylor, and numerous others.

When the bubble burst, and Florida's dazzling real estate boom collapsed, so did the mighty Mizner empire. Creditors took over the Cloister Inn, and Mizner went back to Palm Beach to earn a living as an architect. He died in 1933.

Clarence H. Geist, an Indiana farm boy who made $54 million in public utilities, bought the Cloister Inn in 1928 and expanded it into the fabulous Boca Raton Hotel & Club. It is now owned by the Arvida Corporation.

CAMPBELLTON
Baptist Church
Oldest in Florida

THE OLDEST BAPTIST CHURCH

CAMPBELLTON—The oldest chartered Missionary Baptist Church in Florida is located in Campbellton. It started out with 19 charter members on March 13, 1825, just a short time after Florida became a territory of the United States in 1821.

The pretty white frame church is about a block from the main intersection of the town where U. S. 231 and State Road 2 cross. Campbellton, by the way, is in Jackson County, about five miles from the Florida-Alabama state line. The small agricultural community has 309 inhabitants. It is located within twenty miles of the Alabama town of Dothan.

Throughout the three centuries of Spanish rule in Florida there was little or no Protestant activity in the pioneer state. But as soon as Florida was sold by Spain to the United States for five million dollars, the various Protestant denominations became active. This is when the church, first known as Bethlehem Baptist Church, was started. For the first two years, the congregation had no meeting hall, and the members got together in one another's homes.

The first church building, made of logs, had two front doors and partitions down the center—to separate the sexes. The pews, still in existence even if not in use anymore, were built with heavy straight-backed seats held together by hand-forged iron nails.

Church rules were very strict: a record of three successive absences was grounds for dismissal. The first exclusion of a member for intemperance came in 1827. The first slave was taken into membership in April 1832. Slaves were registered under their given names and as property of their respective owners.

In 1852, the congregation bought ten acres of land at $10 an acre and erected the present central building. It also had two doors and a partition to separate the sexes as well as a balcony for slaves. The name of the church was changed to Campbellton Baptist in 1859. Almost a century later, in 1948, it was remodeled on the inside, and a block of Sunday School rooms added.

A UNION HERO BUILT LIGHTHOUSES IN FLORIDA

CEDAR KEY—One of the heros of the Union army was Lt. Gen. George Gordon Meade, a familiar figure in Florida before the Civil War.

General Meade was with the Topographical Engineer Corps of the U. S. Army and is credited with constructing at least two of the important lighthouses on the coastline of our state. One was at Sand Key not far from Key West, and another at Seahorse Key (*see photo*) near Cedar Key.

The lighthouse at Sand Key was the first screw pile lighthouse in the United States. The whole structure was supported by piles of wrought iron eight inches thick that were screwed into the sea bottom at a depth of ten feet. A fierce hurricane struck Sand Key in 1856 and smashed everything in sight vut the lighthouse.

General Meade, who was a controversial Union commander-in-chief and who had served as a young lieutenant during the Second Seminole War, built the lighthouse on Seahorse Key in 1855. This key is about three miles off Cedar Key which was becoming a prosperous spot at about the same time as pencil manufacturers harvested the abundance of cedar trees growing on the isle. The lighthouse was used as a Federal prison during the Civil War.

COLLIER MEMORIAL

COLLIER-SEMINOLE STATE PARK—The biggest landowner of the biggest county in Florida was the man for whom Collier County was named.

Barron G. Collier, who had accumulated great wealth from street-car advertising in New York and all over the country, was the pioneer empire builder who came to Southwest Florida and started buying up real estate in 1921. He bit off such a chunk of what were then Lee and Hendry Counties that the newly created county was named in his honor. It has been estimated that he owned from 90 to 99 per-cent of the county, and was its largest taxpayer. At the time of his death in 1939, he rated as the largest landowner in Florida. Collier County's 1,300,000 acres make it the largest in size in the state.

The dynamic developer of a wilderness area is appropriately mem-orialized in Collier-Seminole State Park on U. S. 41 south of Naples, the land for which was partly donated by Collier. The park consists of 6,400 acres, much of it in its native state of mangrove jungle. It is just about as far north as the stately Royal Palm may be found in its native habitat, and the area is often referred to as "Royal Palm Hammock."

The magnificent memorial consists of a colonnade and bust of Collier. Flanking the colonnade are tablets mounted on native rock listing the names of Federal troops and Seminole Indians who gave their lives in bloody battles during the Indian wars. Collier's most significant memorial is the lively, vibrant, and prosperous section he he carved out of the Everglades.

THE WORLD'S MOST BEAUTIFUL SWIMMING HOLE

CORAL GABLES—Developers and promoters of Coral Gables during Florida's flamboyant boom days in the 1920s weren't content just to turn an old rock quarry into "the world's most beautiful swimming hole," but dreamed up ingenious stunts to exploit it.

Would you believe Paul Whiteman, the roly-poly moustachioed maestro, leading his jazz band in a bathing suit as the musicians swung out right from the cool waters of the Venetian Pool? And how about the silver-tongued orator, William Jennings Bryan, who was paid $50,000 a year to pitch daily poolside sales speeches? And some of the world's first and most glamorous beauty contests were held on a boardwalk across the pool.

The municipal swimming pool, which attracts 200,000 visitors a year, contains 810,000 gallons of fresh water along with rock towers, caves, arched bridges, a waterfall, islands, and a sandy beach. And there are shady porticos, vine covered loggias, great Spanish towers, and a profusion of palm trees.

A unique and living souvenir is given to visitors of the historic pool: a leaf from an "air plant," known as Cathedral Bells or Kalanchee, which will grow indoors or out, without soil or water. It is a native of Asia.

IT'S "H" AFTER "A," DAYTONA BEACH TIME

DAYTONA BEACH–If it's 20 past 11 o'clock elsewhere, it's "H" after "A" by the quaint landmark tower clock on this, the "world's most famous beach."

The unique face on the timepiece spells out "Daytona Beach," and fun-loving beach-combers seem to like the letters better than the figures. The structure was built in the early 1920s at the same time as the Bandshell and Arcade, shown at left, were erected. The natural building material used was coquina rock, a limestone quarried locally that was formed by atrophied tiny shells in the prehistoric era.

During World War II, the Women's Army Corps was established in this East Coast mecca which was originally founded by a Mathias Day of Mansfield, Ohio, in 1870. He purchased an old Spanish grant containing 3,200 acres for a town site. The village thrived, but Day is said to have lost money on his investment. His name was perpetuated however with "Daytona" winning over "Daytonia" and "Daytown" in a contest.

Actually, the community has a triple waterfront. There's the twenty-three-mile oceanfront, and both banks of the Halifax River.

Daytona was incorporated in 1876, with 23 voters in favor and two against. The town did not blossom until 1890 when the great developer Henry M. Flagler built a bridge across the St. Johns River near Palatka, transformed a primitive railroad into a standard-size one, and extended it southward to Daytona. The Florida East Coast Railroad eventually extended from Jacksonville to Key West.

ROSEBANK

DUNNELLON—He was known far and wide as "The Duke of Dunnellon," the man who accidentally discovered hard rock phosphate at this mining community on May 1, 1889. His name was Albertus Vogt, an adventurer who even was a guerilla fighter after the defeat of the Confederacy.

At one time a surveyor and another time a deputy U. S. marshal, the colorful "Duke" once operated a stage coach between Ocala and Homosassa. He was married to a pretty young widow, Mary Renfro Anderson, in 1886. He already had his home built there in the little community of Renfro, now known as western Dunnellon, and his bride named the estate "Rosebank."

"Rosebank" is still standing today, a weather-beaten, rambling structure with a big yard and lots of shade trees. A description of "Rosebank" in its early days is given by Dunnellon's biographer, J. Lester Dinkins: "Rosebank, built on a knoll overlooking Renfro Springs, was constructed facing South on Old Inglis Road, a road that no longer exists. Sourrounded by gardens, wide piazzas, and well-kept grounds, the structure, with its stained-glass windows, presented passers-by with an impressive appearance.

"The furniture was ornate, ahnd-hewn oak and cedar. Delicately hand-painted lamp globes and china were imported from England and Germany." Rosebank was, indeed, a showplace of Central Florida.

U. D. C. HEADQUARTERS IN "PATTEN HOUSE"

ELLENTON—The Florida Division of the United Daughters of the Confederacy gained a permanent headquarters, and the State of Florida a historic structure with the purchase of the attractive "Patten House."

The building is an excellent example of primitive Florida architecture from the period of around the turn of the century and a valuable addition to the historic Gamble Mansion complex here on U. S. Highway 301, in this village near Bradenton. The Gamble Mansion is the place where Judah P. Benjamin, "the brain of the Confederacy," hid out on his flight from the Federal troops chasing him at the end of the Civil War. The Mansion has been a State Monument for many years.

Maj. George Patten, a wealthy cotton-merchant from Savannah, Georgia, came here after the war and settled his family in the Gamble Mansion. He bought the beautiful property at auction in 1873 for $3,000—fifteen years earlier, the same estate had sold for $190,000. The Pattens lived there a while, but the structure was awfully run down and in need of a new roof and other repairs.

The major decided to build his own cottage and move out of the Gamble Mansion. The family lived happily ever after in the comfortable but modest frame house. A back wing, two bedrooms, and an upstairs balcony were added later. The Mansion stood deserted until the U. D. C. ladies became interested in it and prevailed upon the State to take it over.

After the death of Mrs. Dudley Patten in 1967, the State Parks Board acquired the Patten House for $30,000, and it was moved several hundred yards north to another location on the Mansion grounds. The U. D. C. ladies have done a magnificent job of restoring it and furnishing it with period furniture typical of that used around 1870 or later.

EIGHT FLAGS OVER FORT CLINCH

FERNANDINA BEACH—Anchored at the northeast corner of the Florida peninsula, this interesting and quiet community features century-old Fort Clinch. Eight flags have waved from the fort since its construction began in 1847.

The flags were the following: France (the Huguenots settled here first in 1564, one year before the founding of St. Augustine); Spain (three times); Great Britain; the "Republic of East Florida;" the Green Cross of Florida; Mexico; the Confederate States of America; and, of course, the Stars and Stripes of the United States.

Fort Clinch, located in a beautiful State Park on Amelia Island, was just completed when the Civil War started. The Confederates seized it, but had to give it up, after a struggle in March 1862. Federal troops garrisoned the town for the duration of the war. The bastion was also used during the Spanish-American War in 1898.

Visitors admire the splendid brickwork in the fort, the walls of which are eight feet thick, with the inner walls pierced by tunnels. There is a good museum now inside the fort.

The fort honors the name of Gen. Duncan L. Clinch, a Federal officer during the Seminole War. He had served with distinction in the War of 1812 and also fought in the war with Mexico. The beloved commander retired from the Army and developed a rice plantation in Camden County, Georgia. His business interests included the presidency of the St. Mary's Bank. He also served as a Congressman from Georgia, and once was the Whig candidate for Governor of Georgia.

FLORIDA'S OLDEST SALOON

FERNANDINA BEACH—Old-fashioned swinging doors welcome the thirsty visitor to the Palace Saloon here. It is Florida's oldest bar, built in 1878, and little changed since its construction nearly a century ago. A facade behind the bar was imported from Europe at the time the saloon was established. It is made of hand-carved black oak and two busty, black-oak ladies support it. A carbide lamp hangs overhead and brings back memories of the "good old days." There are hand-painted murals on the walls, painted after the turn of the century, about 1907.

Adding to its decor, the bar has fourteen-pound brass cuspidors. Although heating and air-conditioning were added to the old building in recent times, neither are used very much. Ceiling fans and walls seven bricks thick provide ample insulation. Beveled glass windows also testify to the age of the building.

There was a period in its history when the fancy Palace Saloon could serve the hard stuff for which it was known, namely during Prohibition. It was able to serve it for a while, since the law permitted proprietors to sell all the liquor and beer on hand (and the Palace owners had stocked up well), but then came the long dry spell. For a period, the old saloon, ironically, was turned into an ice cream parlor!

THE "HURRICANE—PROOF" INN

FORT LAUDERDALE—As visionary a man as he was, even Henry Flagler didn't foresee the potential of Fort Lauderdale when he extended his Florida East Coast Railroad southward to Miami in 1895.

This great developer had thought of the vast amount of land he acquired here as farming plots to be sold. Later, Gov. Napoleon Bonparte Broward called this "the richest land this side of the Nile delta." Flagler, who had built hotels all along the East Coast, did not think of New River (as it was known then), as a prospective resort.

But the subcontractor who cleared the right-of-way for the Flagler System later capitalized on the situation. He was Philomen N. Bryan, who built the New River Inn when there were hardly more than one hundred residents here. Concerned about the possibility of hurricanes, Bryan ruled out a frame structure, and erected a three-story concrete-block hotel, using sand from the beach to manufacture the .blocks. This was about 1905.

Word of the "hurricane-proof" hotel got around, and the elegant hostelry was a success from the start. So much so that Tom Bryan, son of the builder, used to meet the 2 a.m. train to warn passengers not to disembark, as there were no vacancies at the Inn.

The handsome hotel boasted carbide lights, a cold-water drinking fountain in the lobby, two bathrooms for its 40 rooms, and its own water and sewage system. One of its noted guests was said to have been President Grover Cleveland. Lately, the building has been used as a City Hall annex, but it is planned to make it a historical museum.

THE WORLD'S "MOST BEAUTIFUL POST OFFICE"

FORT MYERS—The world's "most beautiful post office" isn't a post office anymore. Fort Myers has a new structure for its mail facilities and the one that brought fame to the city now serves other Federal offices.

The handsome building is strictly tropical South Florida. The designer, Nat Gaillard Walker, caused quite a stir in architectural circles when the post office was built during the depression.

The building material used is coral rock, sea shells, and limestone, quarried in the Florida Keys. Across the front of the building runs an open loggia with eight massive stone columns. Behind the columns were mail boxes which could be reached by the holders from the outside.

The site of the post office on West First Street is the location of the first Army post in southwest Florida, way back in the 1840s when this community was known as Fort Harvie.

One of the great admirers of the old structure is Jack Beater, a local author and prolific writer of Florida folklore. In his book *True Tales of the Florida West Coast,* Beater relates his pique over political credit grabbed on the cornerstone of the magnificent building. Beater reported that the post office was authorized and nearly finished as a Public Works Administration project under President Herbert Hoover. The cornerstone, part of the original contract, recognizes the project as a "Republican" job with credit to Hoover and his Postmaster General. But the administration changed before dedication day, and Franklin D. Roosevelt's Postmaster General, Jim Farley, got the credit.

RELICS FROM THE SEA

FORT PIERCE–Look around most any public area in this East coast community and you'll see some interesting relics salvaged from the ocean waters. Back in 1929, a total of 16 cannons and four giant anchors were retrieved. They came from wrecked vessels lying on a reef just north of the city. Local folk were pleased with their find, dressed up the coral-encrusted pieces with aluminum paint, and put them on display. Some relics decorate the little lawn in front of City Hall, others add interest to other parks (such as the one shown in the photo, located on busy U. S. 1 on the southside of town), and before the building of the Chamber of Commerce.

In addition to coral, oyster shells also encrust the relics to such an extent that it has never been fully determined where they came from. It is said that dim mouldings on the cannons indicate that they may have been part of the armament of an early French or Spanish vessel.

The relics may have been part of the equipment on Spanish treasure ships. There was a convoy of eleven ships of the Silver Fleet that sank in the Vero Beach-Fort Pierce area in a hurricane in 1715. The convoy was under command of Captain-General Don Juan Esteban de Ubilla, who was commissioned to bring home to Spain millions of dollars of bullion and other treasures that had piled up in the West Indies during the long War of the Spanish Succession. The fleet sailed from Havana on July 27, 1715. Making its way up the Florida coast, the ships were suddenly struck on July 31 by a violent hurricane. All but one of the vessels were dashed on the reefs between Fort Pierce and Sebastian Inlet. The captain of *La Holandesa,* Sebastian Mendez, led a party by foot to notify the Spanish settlement at St. Augustine of the disaster. Mendez testified that, although he had sailed many years and suffered through many tempests, he had never seen anything as violent as this hurricane.

Recently, professional treasure hunters located the sand-covered wrecks of two of these ships and salvaged many valuable artifacts ranging from cannon to pewter, silver table settings, and jewelry. The rich discovery has been labeled the "Fort Pierce Find."

A FORT BUILT AROUND A LIGHTHOUSE

GARDEN KEY—Way out here in the Dry Tortugas isles, some sixty-nine miles west of Key West in the Gulf of Mexico, is a lighthouse that has been in operation since 1825. It predates the massive Fort Jefferson that surrounds it by twenty years.

For years, this cluster of coral islets was a hangout for pirates. When the United States acquired Florida in 1821, the buccaneers were chased away. Then, for additional insurance to a growing United States commerce in the Gulf, a lighthouse was built on Garden Key. Thirty-one years later, the present 150-foot light on nearby Loggerhead Key was erected.

The contract for lights at Cape Florida, Dry Tortugas, and Sambo Key was awarded to Samuel B. Lincoln of Hingham, Massachusetts, in July 1824. Lincoln was lost at sea on a trip to the Keys shortly thereafter, and his bondsmen were directed to pick up the contract. The lighthouse on Garden Key was constructed, and Keeper William Flaherty arrived with his wife in late 1825.

A spokesman for the U. S. Coast Guard reported that Flaherty's "industry and enthusiasm left something to be desired. He failed to keep his wicks trimmed and the lantern panes were so black no light showed through." It also developed that Mrs. Flaherty was unhappy, fresh provisions did not arrive often enough, and social life was nil. Travel opportunities were restricted, and the mosquitoes terrible. She wrote a letter of complaint to President Adam's wife, and Flaherty was transferred shortly afterwards. When Fort Jefferson was built around the lighthouse, its quarter-acre site remained lighthouse property.

"THE OLD HOUSE"

HERNANDO—Half-a-block off U. S. 41 in this lakeside community north of Inverness is an interesting old house that now serves as an antique shop. But is was originally built during the phosphate boom to provide hotel accommodations.

The two-story frame structure was built by James Ernest Westbrook as a homestead and hotel in 1891. Among its features was an upstairs ballroom, space now filled with artifacts of yesteryear. The Westbrooks has six children, all born in this house.

In the early years there wasn't much activity around Hernando, but the phosphate discovery in 1900 set off a boom, and the first railroad was built. The Westbrooks soon sold the property to the Wilkerson family and moved to Texas. The new owners continued to run a boarding house and hotel until the Westbrooks returned in 1906 and bought back their old place. They resumed operation of the hotel until Westbrook's death in 1920.

Other owners came along, among them a Mr. Hooper who rented rooms and established a well-known dining room. People came from miles around to enjoy the delicious meals, especially the Sunday dinners.

Finally, Harold Fowler purchased the home place, closed the hotel and used it as a dwelling. It is now owned by Mrs. Evelyn Ferguson, formerly of St. Petersburg, and used as a museum and antique shop.

The landmark is usually referred to as "The Old House," as good an appellation as any.

MONUMENT TO UNREQUITED LOVE

HOMESTEAD—Some say that Edward Leedskalnin built the bizarre coral castle alongside busy U. S. 1 here to furnish a home for the girl of his dreams—a girl he never met. Others say he fled to America in the first place because he had been jilted on his wedding day back in his native Latvia, and that he erected the massive fortress-like home hoping that one day his "ex," whom he called "Sweet Sixteen," would come.

At any rate, he was unlike the poet who wanted to live in his house by the side of the road "and be a friend of man." Leedskalnin was a recluse who first constructed a gigantic eight-foot stone wall around his castle site to keep prying eyes away.

The coral curtain cloaked the work of the diminutive 97-pound immigrant with a veil that not even death itself has been able to brush aside. Before his death in 1951, Leedskalnin never revealed how he was able to move the huge coral rocks weighing up to 35 tons which he excavated single-handedly. He boasted he knew the secrets used in building the pyramids of Egypt. It is known that he used primitive tools; his brace and bit was the crank of a Model T Ford.

Notable features of the castle include a nine-ton swinging door so perfectly pivoted that a child can turn it. There is also a great obelisk weighing twenty-eight and a half tons. A bowl-shaped sundial marks the time accurately and adjusts itself to the seasons, which is all the more remarkable because its builder had no more than a fourth-grade education.

FREDERICK DELIUS IN FLORIDA

JACKSONVILLE—The shady banks of the beautiful St. John's River and the serenity of the northeast Florida countryside provided the backdrop Frederick Delius needed to ignite his tremendous musical career.

He disappointed his father but pleased the whole world when he spurned the life of a businessman and developed into a great composer. And it all started here in Florida.

Delius's father was a wealthy tool merchant in Bradford, England. He tried to interest his son in the same enterprise, but Frederick was not interested. His father decided to send the young man to faraway Florida to operate an orange grove that he was buying for the rebellious youth.

So in the spring of 1884, Frederick Delius took a boat ride up the St. John's from Jacksonville to the tiny community of Picolata on State Road 13. There he built a little four-room house with a kitchen connected by a covered walk. He soon forgot his mission to make money on oranges; the freeze of 1895 wiped out the trees, and he, therefore, addressed himself to his first love, music. He had a teacher from Jacksonville, Thomas F. Ward, come and live in the cottage where he got his basic instruction. Here Delius composed his soon-to-be-famous "Florida Suite," which he dedicated to "The People of Florida."

Delius told a friend back in England that "in Florida, through sitting and gazing at nature, I gradually learned the way in which I should find myself." He died in 1934 at the age of 72. His cottage was restored and moved to Jacksonville University.

CONVENT SERVED AS HOSPITAL

KEY WEST—Until its razing in recent times, the Convent of Mary Immaculate was one of the historic landmarks in this historic city. The beautiful building stood next to St. Mary's Star of the Sea Roman Catholic Church on Truman Avenue.

The old convent was built by the Sisters of the Holy Names of Jesus and Mary, a Canadian order which first established a school in Key West in 1868, shortly after the Civil War. This building was erected in 1878. The odd architectural design was by William Kerr of Ireland and is of Romanesque style, with dormered mansard roofs and a central tower. The building was enlarged in 1904. Mr. Kerr also designed three public buildings, the old Post Office, the old City Hall, and the Monroe County Court House.

During the Spanish-American War, when Key West was a center of activity for troops headed for Cuba or returning, the Sisters offered their services as nurses and the Convent to the U. S. Navy as a hospital. The Sisters rendered devoted service to the wounded and to the victims of yellow fever.

In 1901, Sister Egidius started a museum at the Convent. It contained a large collection of artifacts of the Spanish-American War as well as items from the Civil War and from World Wars I and II.

A special item of interest at the museum was a shell-encrusted chest made by Dr. Samuel A. Mudd during his imprisonment at Fort Jefferson, sixty-nine miles west of Key West in the Dry Tortugas. Mudd had been convicted as a Lincoln conspirator after treating John Wilkes Booth's broken leg.

"FLAGLER'S FOLLY"

KEY WEST—The unique Overseas Highway, the "highway that goes to sea," is a two-lane bridge-and-causeway combination that stretches for some 159 miles from Miami to Key West.

Key West is the southern end of U. S. 1 which terminates up north at Kent, Maine. The Overseas Highway, which provides an eye-filling tour from coral key to coral key, handles a heavy concentration of motor vehicles now. Yet originally it was the roadbed for the rails of the old Florida East Coast Railroad Extension.

Henry Flagler, the great Florida developer who had leap-frogged down the east coast, building railroads and elegant hotels, and one final ambition in life: to extend the FEC into Key West. It was a dangerous and expensive venture, and his scoffers called it "Flagler's Folly." Hurricane after hurricane struck his dedicated work force of 5,000 men. Finally, the Overseas Railroad was completed and presented to Flagler as a birthday present in January 1912. Some 700 men lost their lives working on the job which took seven years and nine months of heroic effort and engineering ingenuity. It cost fifty million dollars. Flagler died a year later at the age of 84.

The railroad continued to operate until a mighty hurricane hit the Keys on Labor Day in 1935. The storm swept away forty-one miles of tracks and trestles, and washed away many miles of fill. Railroad officials decided not to rebuild. An Overseas Highway and Bridge District was formed which eventually transformed the railroad bed into a roadway which was formally opened in 1944.

JOSEPH YATES PORTER, M.D.

KEY WEST—The handsome ante-bellum home at Caroline and Duval streets, with its cool verandahs and gingerbread trimmings, is typical Key West architecture. It is also a historic structure.

For it was in this house that Dr. Joseph Yates Porter was born, lived, and died. He was born there on October 21, 1847, and he died on March 16, 1927 in the same room in which he was born 80 years ago.

The Florida Medical Association is not often given to superlatives in referring to physicians, but Dr. Porter stands out as such a hero in Florida's medical history. He deserves the flowery inscription on a marker erected by the F. M. A. at the Porter House in May 1968. It proclaims:

". . . First health officer of the State of Florida, 1889-1917. Thirteenth President of the Florida Medical Association. Under his far-sighted leadership, yellow fever and other epidemic diseases were eradicated. Perhaps no other person has exerted more influence upon the health of this state that Dr. Porter."

The famous Floridian earned his doctorate in medicine at Jefferson Medical College in Philadelphia in 1870. According to the Florida State Board of Health, "the year of his graduation he was appointed acting assistant surgeon of the U. S. Army and was assigned to Fort Jefferson in Dry Tortugas where the martyred Dr. Mudd served so nobly." He spent 19 years in the Army Medical Corps.

Dr. Porter was the first State health officer, a post he held for 28 years. He gained fame fighting "yellowjack" or yellow fever in the 1880s.

"OLD 91"

KEY WEST—The handsome Romanesque red-brick building domina-ting Mallory Square in downtown Key West is lovingly called "Old 91," for it was built in 1891 as the local Customs and Post Office building. The landmark was added to the National Register of Histor-ic places in 1973.

"Old 91" is presently a part of the Naval Station property and houses the Industrial Relations office. But it is being declared sur-plus. It was used as the Navy's administration offices from 1935 to 1947, and during World War I it served as an administration central for the armed forces.

Key West's Post Office was established in 1829, and the mail was brought here by a small sailing vessel which plied between here and Charleston, South Carolina. The community was a busy port in those days. In 1831, the Customs Service listed imports worth $115,710 for Florida—and Key West's share of this business was 87%!

In the early days, the Key Westers became prosperous salvaging valuable cargo from wrecked ships along the rugged shores of the Florida Keys. It was so lucrative that Key West was said to have the greatest wealth per capita of any city in the United States in 1834. Salvaged goods were brought to Key West and auctioned off in an old warehouse.

As soon as Florida became a part of the United States, the Feder-al Government began erecting a network of lighthouses along its long coastline. The lighthouses provided navigational aid for ships, and made shipping safe along the Keys. Thus, the wrecking of ships di-minished.

THE WORLD'S MOST UNIQUE MONUMENT

KISSIMMEE–An unusual "Monument of States" in Lake Front Park here was an imaginative creation as a do-it-yourself project by the Kissimmee All States Tourist Club.

Billed as "the world's most unique monument," the shaft was two years in the building. The tourists themselves did all the labor. There was no paid archutect, no paid cement finisher, no paid contractor no paid stone mason or stone engraver.

The tower is in the form of an irregular quadrilateral step-pyramid Of 21 varying tiers. It reaches 50 feet in the air, with a flag pole extending further upward.

More than 1500 stones from every state in the Union and from 21 foreign countries went into the odd structure. President Franklin D. Roosevelt sent a stone from the wall of his Hyde Park Estate, Prime Minister MacKenzie King one from Canada, and Gov. Rexford Guy Tugwell one from Puerto Rico. Stones from the states were sent by their governors. The Victory Walk encircling the structure cites the names of donors of one or more bags of cement, inscribed in concrete.

The stone collection is a geologist's dream. Included are quartz, marble, granite, agate, flint, alabaster, coquina, meteors, stalagmites, petrified teeth, lava, and many mineral ores.

The monument was dedicated on March 28, 1943, by the eloquent Claude Pepper, then U. S. Senator from Florida, who is now a member of Congress.

FRANK LLOYD WRIGHT

LAKELAND—Frank Lloyd Wright had a field day at Florida Southern College, a Methodist-related institution here.

The late Dr. Ludd M. Spivey, president of the college for thirty-two years, "sold" the noted architect on designing the "College of Tomorrow" here, and then turned him loose. The then-67-year-old creator and expounder of "organic architecture" launched a building program of eighteen modern buildings. Organic architecture was his term for buildings that harmonize with users and environment. Thus Lakeland acquired the largest concentration of Frank Lloyd Wright architecture in the world.

The basic materials in his plan for Florida Southern were steel for strength, sand because it was Florida, and glass to bring God's outdoors into man's indoors. The campus sprawls on a hillside overlooking Lake Hollingsworth, in a citrus-grove setting.

The cornerstone for the first building, the Annie Pfeiffer Chapel (shown in photo), was laid in 1938. This creation of the foremost non-conformist attracted countless people to Lakeland to see Wright's work.

One innovation of the imaginative architect was the "esplanade" which furnishes a sheltered promenade between buildings. Wright, who designed Tokyo's Imperial Hotel and other famous structures throughout the world, inserted small, colored glass squares into the block walls so that, during daytime, colored sunshine may stream into the buildings, a bit of God's outdoors in man's indoors.

A LONELY, ELDERLY "PRINCESS"

LAKE WALES–Once upon a time there was a wealthy Minneapolis banker named Irwin A. Yarnell. He came to Florida in the early 1920s and developed Highlands Park and Crooked Lake subdivisions here. With him came his wife Josephine who became one of Florida's most socially prominent women. She was a princess in the eyes of her rich husband who built her a castle in Mediterranean-style architecture high on a hill overlooking a lake in Highland Park. It was named *Casa de Josefina*, "The House of Josephine," in her honor.

The Casa was one of Florida's showplaces. Centered on a 26-acre estate, it had one of the most complete botanical gardens anywhere. Every species of palm tree known was planted there.

The "princess" and her husband toured the world to fill their home with priceless antiques, such as chairs from the time of Caesar, tapestries and rugs from Moslem harems, and paintings by the Old Masters.

But the bubble burst. Mr. Yarnell lost millions, but managed to retain the Casa. The couple continued to live there, and reared its family of three daughters. Mr. Yarnell died in 1936, the children married and left, and the "princess" was alone in her castle.

The story skips to 1954 when local tongues began wagging. Widow Yarnell, then 68, was marrying a young Prince Charming. The bridegroom was Clarence J. Tibado, 33, a native of Lake Wales and a promising artist. During World War II, he served on the *USS Pensacola,* and men on the ship commissioned him to paint fifteen major battles in which the ship participated. He came back to Lake Wales, his casual acquaintance with Mrs. Yarnell blossomed into a full romance, and they were wed.

Recently, the Casa, vacated a few years ago, was turned into a club house for La Casa condominiums.

MORE BEAUTIFUL AND BETTER

LAKE WALES—Edward W. Bok's grandfather chased away pirates from a grim island in the North Sea, turned it into "a bower of green verdure and trees" to which came the birds who made it famous forever as the "Island of Nightingales."

The grandfather raised trees and the grandmother raised children. She also raised the sights of her offspring with such admonitions as "Make you the world a bit better and more beautiful because you have lived in it."

At the age of six, the little Dutch boy was brought to America. As a youngster, he scrubbed windows at fifty cents per week to aid his struggling family. He rose to become one of the country's leading journalists, as the crusading editor of the *Ladies Home Journal* and in other capacities. In 1920 he wrote his autobiography, *The Americanization of Edward Bok,* which won the Pulitzer Prize.

Bok was grateful to the nation in which he made his mark. Here in Lake Wales, in the highlands of Florida, he found a spot to establish a sanctuary "for humans and birds." And then he built the Singing Tower, a magnificent structure atop the highest hill in Florida. The 205-foot tower was designed by architect Milton B. Medary, while the landscape artist was Fredrick Law Olmsted. Bok's good friend, President Calvin Coolidge, dedicated the tower on February 1, 1929. It is often called "America's Taj Mahal."

The tower, an original concept, not a copy, rates with two other great works—the Nebraska State Capitol and the Kansas City Liberty Memorial. Those structures caught and expressed the spirit of the prairie, while Bok's tower rings out the spirit of tropical Florida. The noted editor is buried beneath the lawn at the foot of the tower.

GRANT DIDN'T SLEEP HERE

LONGWOOD—Passers-by used to whiz through the village of Alta-monte Springs on State Road 436 near Interstate 4, and spy an interesting old house by the side of the road. The pulse of a history buff quickened when local folk repeated the rumor that the house was built by Gen. Ulysses S. Grant, the former president, and that this is where he wrote his memoirs.

A check in the library of the *Orlando Sentinel-Star* yielded a clipping saying this was indeed "General Grant's house." But digging deeper into the files, subsequent news stories turn up to debunk the Grant story. An enterprising reporter talked to the General's grand-son, retired Army Maj. Gen. U. S. Grant III who stated flatly that the story is not true.

Be that as it may, the house itself is still interesting. The twelve-room, three-story structure was swallowed up by a thicket of trees and shrubbery. Its cupolas are reminiscent of past grandeur. The Grant story was started, according to one theory, by an alleged social climber who was trying to sell the house—thus the name-dropping.

The old house was probably built along with other similarly or-nate structures back in the s870s near a fashionable resort hotel of the day, known as the Altamonte Hotel.

General Grant did visit Florida after retiring—but it is doubtful he stopped off at Altamonte, let alone built a house there.

In 1973, the Central Florida Society of Historic Preservation ac-quired the "Grant House" lock, stock, and barrel and moved it to the near-by village of Longwood, to become an integral part of a museum of homes. It now sits on West Warren Avenue facing the Village Square, opposite the historic Longwood Hotel.

THE BLOCKHOUSE BUILT IN 1837

MacCLENNY—Deep in the heart of the backwoods here in Baker County stands truly a historical gem. It is the last relic of its kind in Florida, a blockhouse built during the Second Seminole War to protect white residents from attacks by Indians.

An authority on the structure is a native of Baker County, Edwin J. Fraser, former State Senator and former Secretary of the State Senate. He says the main body of this house was built by Jim Burnsed in the year 1837. He sold this place about 1866 to Hugh Brown. Carl Brown, a son of Hugh Brown and a distant relative of Fraser, raised his family there and the place is now known as the "ole Carl Brown place." ·

The original structure is still basically good and sound. The people of MacClenny are hopeful some group will act to preserve this historical landmark, which they say reveals "so much of our rich history." It has been suggested that the blockhouse be moved and reconstructed in MacClenny, which sits on U. S. 90 west of Jacksonville, or at the Civil War battleground site at Olustee, so it could be viewed more easily by the curious public.

It is built of hewn, rich pine logs dovetailed at the corners and put together with wooden pegs, and with loop holes cut between the logs to aim rifles through.

One pointed post still standing indicates that originally the blockhouse was in a compound with many pointed posts, higher than a man's head surrounding it. When the Indians were on the warpath, the whites would gather here and stay until things settled down.

The Seminoles were too shrewd to attack blockhouses. They waited for the whites to leave these compounds, and then jumped them from ambush.

Many years ago there were numerous blockhouses such as this one in Baker County. But it is suspected that this is the only remaining one not only in Florida, but possibly in the entire Southeast.

THAT "LITTLE WOMAN WHO STARTED A GREAT BIG WAR"

MANDARIN—Abraham Lincoln called her "that little woman who started a great big war." And after Harriet Beecher Stowe had written the world-wide bestseller *Uncle Tom's Cabin,* her name was anathema in Dixie.

But the gifted writer became one of Florida's most distinguished residents, and a drum-beater for the Sunshine State far more than the most exuberant Chamber-of-Commerce press agent.

The Stowe family came to this picturesque spot on the St. Johns River below Jacksonville in 1867, during Reconstruction days. Both her husband, clergyman Calvin Ellis Stowe, and her son Frederick, had health problems. Her prolific and imaginative pen made her the breadwinner.

The famous author was the No. 1 attraction for travelers aboard the riverboats passing her home in Mandarin. The old home was destroyed by fire a few years ago, but the carriage house shown in the photo still stands on property owned by retired Pan Am and Navy pilot Carl F. Tauch. It has been remodeled into a handsome guest house, but originally provided shelter for five carriages on the ground floor, while the upper floor had been a nicely-furnished apartment for Negro footmen.

Here, amid the orange trees, live oaks, birds, animals, and the river, Mrs. Stowe wrote *Palmetto Leaves* in 1873, a volume of tranquil sketches describing the area and boosting Florida. Her other writings of the period were, for the most part, violent polemics.

"ROOM & BOARD, $2—YOU FURNISH MEAT"

MARCO ISLAND—An early tariff schedule for the old Marco Island Inn here tells of $2 per day room rates with dinner at 6 P.M. sharp for those who provided their own fish or fowl.

This ancient hostelry, still doing business at the same old stand nearly one hundred years after its erection, is truly a landmark on colorful Marco Island. The island underwent a face-lifting when the sophisticated Mackle Brothers developed an attractive retreat area in the 1960s and 1970s.

The historic inn was originally constructed in 1883 by Capt. W. D. (Bill) Collier, son of an early pioneer, and it was then called the Marco Hotel. All of the material for the building was brought in by schooner from Boca Grande, then the nearest railroad terminal. In fact, the only way of reaching Marco Island in those days was by water. The old hotel had twenty sleeping rooms, a parlor, a dining room, and a bathroom. Bill Collier operated the hotel, complete with dock and trading post, for several years.

Some years later, George Ruppert, brother of Jacob Ruppert of the New York beer and baseball family, purchased the building with his in-law, a Mrs. Erickson, and turned it into a private fishing lodge. George Ruppert died in 1942, during World War II. Later in the war, the United States Armed Forces took over the Inn, constructed near-by barracks and a dock, and turned it into an air-sea rescue base for crash boats operating in the Gulf of Mexico. In 1946, a syndicate leased the property from the Ruppert estate and opened the building again as a commercial hotel, the Marco Island Inn.

A previously obscure aspect of the old inn was uncovered during a recent remodeling when an array of antique bottles was discovered under the attic floorboards. How many remember the likes of "Old Malurey Export Whiskey" or "Monograph High Grade Celebrated Alcohol?"

BUILT TO LAST FOR CENTURIES

MIAMI—William Jennings Bryan was the best salesman a town ever had. Coral Gables paid the great orator and three-time candidate for President of the United States $50,000 a year to stand beside the Venetian Pool and make such claims as this: "You can wake up in the morning and tell the biggest lie you can think of about the future of Coral Gables—and before you go to bed at night, you will be ashamed of your modesty."

But Bryan himself lived in Miami, several miles away from the boom-town of Coral Gables. As early Miamians go, he was virtually a pioneer, having built a fine mansion at 3115 Brickell Avenue (see photo) in 1911. This of course was many years before Coral Gables was ever dreamed of. And it was five years before James Deering would build the magnificent Vizcaya on land adjacent to Bryan's place.

The statesman called his place Villa Serena. It is a two-story house of Spanish-type architecture, with a large amount of living space and five bedrooms. Many famous people used to visit the Bryans in Miami, including President Harding.

Mrs. Bryan said she looked around Tampa, Orlando, and elsewhere before she discovered Miami and the lovely homesite in what was then known as Brickell's Hammock.

Mrs. Bryan told about the solid concrete structure with steel rods when she wrote in 1931 that "Mr. Bryan said he would build there a house that would last for centuries." She was proud that the house just recently had survived two ferocious hurricanes that had struck Miami in the 1920s.

The Bryans bought the tract of land on Biscayne Bay for $30,000. When it last changed hands in 1971, it brought $275,000.

LURED WITH ORANGE BLOSSOMS

MIAMI—The combination of fragrant orange blossoms and a woman's flair for dramatic public relations brought Henry Flagler and his railroad to Miami, and it became the turning point in the history of the "Magic City."

The woman with vision was widowed Mrs. Julia Tuttle, who came here in 1891 from Cleveland, Ohio, and bought lands of the defunct Biscayne Bay Company, She tried her best to interest the outside world in Miami. Particularly did she woo Henry Flagler to extend his railroad from Daytona Beach southward. When he wasn't moved, Providence stepped in.

The Great Freeze hit in the winter of 1894-1895, the worst in one hundred years. North Florida suffered under a devastating nineteen-degree temperature, and vegetables and coconut palms as fas as south as Palm Beach were killed. Flagler was in the depths of despair over what appeared to be nature's cancellation of his plans for a great tourist and citrus development.

The ingenious Mrs. Tuttle finally got his attention: she sent Flagler a box of orange blossoms, undamaged by the frost, from Biscayne Bay, and renewed her proposal to give the developer land if he would build a railroad to Miami. This got action. Florida East Coast Railroad was extended to Palm Beach and Miami. Mrs. Tuttle gave Flagler much valuable land, including 100 acres on which the fabulous Royal Palm Hotel was built by Flagler.

Thus, Mrs. Tuttle became known as "the Mother of Miami." This pioneer is buried in a prominent spot in the City Cemetery at North-East Eighteenth Street and Second Avenue. The Thirty-Sixth Street Causeway connecting Miami with Miami Beach is named in her honor. Mrs. Tuttle died in 1898, and Miami was on the move—thanks to her orange blossom trick.

"THE ABODE OF THREE LOVES"

MIAMI—Tokyo industrialist Kiyoshi Ischimura is a hard-boiled businessman (the *New York Times* cites him as one of three men who most spurred Japanese post-war growth), and a sentimental one.

A frequent visitor here, he fell in love with Miami and wanted to show his fondness. The result is an unusual attraction, a delightful Japanese Teahouse and Garden on Watson Island, at the western end of MacArthur Causeway, opposite the Heliport and Blimp base.

The facility is named San-Ai-An, "the abode of three loves." This is explained to mean the love of one's country, one's fellow man, and the love of the work in which one is engaged.

Ischimura started his contributions to the project in 1955, donating several hundred wild orchid trees, and a large 300-year-old Japanese stone lantern. Later he sent an eight-foot, eight-ton granite statue of Hotei, the Japanese deity of good fortune. The authentic teahouse was prefabricated in Japan by six carpenters whose work has been described as the "neatest piece of carpentry ever seen in this area."

The late Robert King High, long-time Mayor of Miami, accepted the gifts and extolled the artistry of the garden and its significance as a symbol of international amity between Japan and the United States.

Mayor High observed: "Mr. Ischimura has bridged the vast expanse of time and distance which separates the cultures of our two nations. East meets West here in the Garden, which expresses an ancient philosophy too seldom understood or appreciated in the twentieth century."

RETREAT FOR A GANGSTER

MIAMI BEACH—Al Capone once said: "I have a wife and a boy I idolize and a beautiful home at Palm Island, Florida. If I could go there and forget it all I would be the happiest man in the world."

There is no doubt that his home at 93 Palm Island in Biscayne Bay is a magnificent mansion. It was one of his rewards for becoming king of the underworld in Chicago back in the Roaring Twenties.

The luxurious abode was built in 1922 for Clarence M. Busch of the brewery family. "Scarface" Capone arranged to buy the estate while he was a prisoner serving a Federal sentence for income tax evasion in the late 1920s. "The Big Fellow," as he was called by his associates, moved into the Florida retreat in 1930. Well-armed body-guards and sentries always were on hand to make it hot for any snoopers or prowlers or revenge-seekers.

Capone added a swimming pool and a two-story cabana to the property. The mobster passed away in this secluded paradise in 1947. The bedroom where he died is said to be just as it was when Capone lived there.

The fabulous stucco castle was put up for sale in 1967. Though Capone had many possessions and loved ones, it is doubtful he ever found the peace which he professed to seek when he tried to get out of the rackets.

LIVE OAK AVENUE

MONTICELLO—"A lover of Nature" was the simple epitaph paying tribute to the late John Howard Girardeau, an early Florida educator, on a marker underneath the giant arms of the trees on Live Oak Avenue here.

The monument was erected by the Girardeau children and dedicated to the memory of the man who planted the live oaks back in 1889. The moss-draped limbs clasp overhead to form a shady canopy and give Monticello a famed beauty spot. Girardeau became County School Superintendent of Jefferson County in 1897 at a time when this community was a cultural and educational center in Florida.

The elegant live oak is an impressive trade mark for the Southland and is the State Tree of Georgia, whose southern border touches this county. The tree takes its name from its own leaves, which are always shine, fresh-looking, and alive, and is classified as an evergreen. Live oak timber is the toughest of woods and the heaviest of oaks, 60 pounds to the cubic foot. It is so hard that it turns the edge of tools when dry.

Back in the olden days, before the days of steel bottoms, the live oak was this country's most prized ship timber. The wood from St. Simon's Island, Georgia, not too far from this North Florida town, was used in the construction of the hull of the frigate *Constitution,* the famed "Old Ironsides" of Oliver Wendell Holmes' poem.

LOUISVILLE PUBLISHER PIONEERED NAPLES

NAPLES—Walter N. Haldeman, who was owner and publisher of the Louisville, Kentucky, *Courier-Journal*, is credited with being the "discoverer" and founder of this lovely city on the lower Gulf coast. Together with nearly a dozen others, Haldeman was first associated as a partner in the Naples Town Improvement Company founded in 1887 to develop the community.

The old publisher would not recognize it today, but his beloved Florida home still stands, located on the beach at 13th Avenue South. It has been kept updated, modernized, and remodeled through the years and is as attractive a retreat now as it was in the pioneer days when the only transportation to Naples was via boat.

The founding group included Gen. John S. Williams, also a Kentuckian and a Confederate Army officer who liked the warm climate here and envisioned the possibility of growing two crops of tobacco a year. It never produced that, but the land was developed by Williams and his cohorts. Haldeman had first spotted this exotic site in 1885 and decided it would make a fine resort. Others interested in Naples in those pioneer days included the famous editor of the *Courier-Journal*, Henry ("Marse Henry") Watterson.

The real estate company built the Naples Hotel in 1889. A pier was built on the site where the present modern pier stretches 1,000 feet into the Gulf waters. The first pier was not an accommodation for anglers so much as it was a wharf for freight and passenger boats, the town's only link with the outside world.

THE GRAVE IN THE MIDDLE OF THE STREET

NEW SMYRNA BEACH—Canova Drive here is a narrow little street. It is named for the brother of singer Judy Canova, a former landowner in the area, but is best-known because motorists have to go around an "island" in the middle of the road.

The island is the grave of 16-year-old Charles Dummett, son of a pioneer citrus grower. The lad, who was fatally wounded in a hunting accident, was the only son of Capt. Douglas D. Dummett (sometimes spelled "Dummitt"), a member of Florida's Citrus Hall of Fame because he was regarded as the "Father of the Indian River citrus industry."

Captain Dummett had come to this country in 1807 from Barbados Island. In St. Augustine he married a socially prominent woman, but she deserted him. He moved to this section, a part of what was known then as Mosquito County. Here the Captain married a young Negro slave girl, Anna. He became noted for fighting Indians as commander of the "Mosquito Roarers" in the Seminole wars. He also served in the Territorial Legislature.

The couple had three daughters and young Charles. The youth was home for Easter holidays from school up North when the tragedy occurred on April 23, 1860. Captain Dummett sadly buried his only son on the property. A marble slab marks the grave. The Dummett family later moved to Merritt Island where the captain developed the fine Indian River orange.

When Canova Drive was built, the engineers left the grave of Charles Dummett untouched.

ORLANDO'S 100th-BIRTHDAY PRESENT

ORLANDO—Orlandoans, who are enterprising, civic-minded people, wanted to do something spectacular to celebrate the 100th birthday anniversary of the "City Beautiful" in 1957, and so they did!

On the big day, October 5, 1957, the gorgeous Orlando Centennial Fountain sprung into action. The fabulous fount with its ever-changing lights at night and its dancing waters by day offers a breath-taking sight to visitors passing Lake Eola near downtown.

The waters spew skyward from an elaborate rig that cost $160,000. It uses 6,200 gallons of water per minute while in operation (the water is pumped from the lake and then returned to it) and it concludes its color cycle in 10 minutes. Sixty-four red, blue, and amber flood lights are located underneath the plexiglas dome in the center of the fountain.

Orlando's birthday gift was the realization of an idea that originated when four local businessmen attended a convention in Washington, D. C., saw the Sheraton Plaza's 50-foot illuminated sprouts of water, and came back home wondering if this city couldn't have something as beautiful. The Chamber of Commerce men were George Sipple, Stuart Johnson, Earl Brown, and Bill Davis. They got the ball rolling, and the fountain was ready to go on Centennial Day.

Waters from the fountains of five nations were poured into the Orlando fountain at the opening ceremony, recognizing the nations that have ruled Florida—Spain, England, the Confederacy, France, and the United States.

"NEIGHBOR JOHN" DISPENSED SHINY DIMES

ORMOND BEACH—John D. Rockefeller, who founded Standard Oil Company and became super-wealthy, spent 23 winters here, from 1914 until his death in 1937.

He came to this pleasant East coast resort on the recommendation of research scientists who proclaimed Ormond such a healthful place that the oil tycoon could fulfill his ambition to live to be 100 years old. He missed the mark by slightly more than two years.

At first, Rockefeller stayed at the swank hotel of his ex-partner Henry M. Flagler, the Ormond Hotel, where he leased a complete floor for the season. Then, he purchased in 1918 the modest estate of Dr. Harwood Huntington, situated across the street from the hotel on Riverside Drive. The Casements, as it was named, wasn't a pretentious place, a house of grey shingles with dark green-and-white awnings on the numerous windows. (Today the home has been converted into a retirement home for senior citizens.)

"Neighbor John," as he was known, was a familiar figure in Ormond Beach. He presided over the annual Charity Bazaar at the hotel; he played golf as long as he was able to do so; and he entertained a few friends in his home. On Sundays, the Standard Oil genius attended the nondenominational Ormond Union Church. In his earlier years he had been a teacher and youth leader at Erie Street Baptist Church in Cleveland, Ohio. After church here, Rockefeller would stand on the lawn and hand out shiny dimes to the children—along with a brief sermon on thrift and saving.

THE ORMOND HOTEL

ORMOND BEACH—The rambling old wooden structure today is said to be the "world's largest hotel for the retired," but at one time it was a swinging place, the capital of the wealthy. It's the Ormond Hotel.

One of the largest wooden-frame hostelries in the world, this elegant building with the huge verandahs was built in 1887 and opened on January 1, 1888, just as civilization was spreading this far south in pioneer Florida.

A syndicate of fifteen investors, headed by pioneer citizens John Anderson and Joseph Price, envisioned this wonderful spot as a coming resort area and gambled on the handsome hotel. The world did not beat a path to their door, mainly because of poor transportation.

To the financial rescue came Henry M. Flagler, the great developer who had just opened the magnificent Ponce de Leon Hotel in Saint Augustine and had started his railroad down the East coast. He bought a large piece of the Ormond Hotel in the 1890s and enlarged it. One attraction added was a golf course, and there was already the famous beach.

The Astors, Vanderbilts, Fords, and numerous other wealthy families took the lure and came. John D. Rockefeller and his entourage rented an entire floor of the hotel in 1914. The well-to-do began building mansions here, and Ormond was said to be one of the richest resort colonies in the world. The hotel was the scene of many charity bazaars—with John D. himself presiding over them.

TOMOKIE THE TIMUCUAN

ORMOND BEACH—When Ponce de Leon landed on the upper East coast of Florida in 1513, his first contact with the natives was with the Timucuan tribe in this region. Their leader was a young and handsome chief named Tomokie who was said to have "the dignity of manners worth of a Roman senator."

Today, Chief Tomokie is honored with a statue that dominates Tomoka State Park, two miles north of Ormond Beach on the Old Dixie Highway. Near the base of the statue is the figure of Oleeta, who, legend has it, slew him in defense of the golden cup.

This heroic group was designed and executed by the Florida artist and sculptor, the late Fred Dana Marsh, and was presented to Florida by him and friends of the park. The park features the Fred Dana Marsh Museum with exhibits and artifacts of Florida geology, zoology, and history. It depicts both the nature and artistic backgrounds of Florida, and thus is unique among museums in the state.

The memorial to Chief Tomokie is at the location of the site of Nocoroco, a famous Indian village which was known to early travelers. It was here that the Timucuans made their last stand against the overwhelming encroachment of the white man. White man's diseases and battles with the Greeks finally brought about the almost total extinction of the Timucuans, 75 years after the arrival of the Spaniards.

Chief Tomokie lamented: "How strange are the ways of the white man. He wears clothes, he builds houses so strong, and lives so short a time. He steals our women, he speaks no truth. Nevertheless, I have ordered my people to be tolerant of the heathen and ungodly paleface, because he knows not of our Great Spirit who tells us to speak the truth. . . ."

STEAMBOATING ON THE ST. JOHN'S RIVER

PALATKA—She looks sad, wallowing there on the banks of the Saint John's River at Hart's Point, rotting away, quietly awaiting final burial on the banks of the beautiful river where she once so proudly sailed.

She's the *Hiawatha,* the last and finest of the Hart Line steamboats that many years ago plied the St. John's, Oklawaha, and Silver rivers, transporting excited visitors from the North to get their first peek at Silver Springs.

The *Hiawatha* is shown here several years ago when she was in better condition than today. The remains are berthed on private property, and boaters on the river can hardly see the famous vessel because of the thick foliage and growth that obscures her.

Steam navigation on the Oklawaha began shortly before the Civil War, but grew in popularity in the post-bellum days when the Northerners first "discovered" Florida as a tourist attraction. Stepping in to provide the steamboats was a former Vermonter, Capt. Hubbard L. Hart, who developed a whole fleet of ships for this purpose.

The *Hiawatha* didn't come along until 1904, and was the largest and finest of the fleet. She had an enrolled length of 89 feet and accommodated 80 first-class passengers and 10 deck passengers. Capacity was maximized by high beam-to-length ratios—29:100 on the *Hiawatha,* with a 25:100 average on the seven major boats.

The *Hiawatha* was built in the same style as two other Hart liners, the *Okeehumkee* and the *Astatula.* She boasted a small fantail deck abaft the upper cabin and carried two stacks placed abreast on the forward part of the upper cabin roof. Ten staterooms on her saloon deck and eighteen on her upper deck made her a first-class passenger boat. Her dining room was on the saloon deck forward, just beneath the pilot house. Communication between the two cabin decks was via a staircase in the aft part of the saloon.

According to Ella Teague deBerard, author of "Steamboating in the Hyacinths," the *Hiawatha* left Palatka at 12:45 p.m. and arrived at Sliver Springs before noon the following day.

BETHESDA-BY-THE-SEA

PALM BEACH—The Church of Bethesda-by-the-Sea, the popular house of worship for America's high society, had a humble beginning when there was a sparse number of white people in southeast Florida.

In 1889, there was no church building in all of Dade County, and there was no "Palm Beach" either. Site of the present wealthy community was then Lake Worth, and this area was part of Dade County which stretched from the St. Lucie River at the north end to the Florida Keys at the south end. Its population in 1880 was 257, and by 1889 a "population explosion" had more than doubled the head count to 600 in the county.

The Rev. Joseph N. Mulford, Rector of Christ Church in Troy, New York, volunteered to come to this wilderness area to start a mission. He began holding services in the District School House, first school house in the county which is now preserved in Phipps Park. It was Mrs. Mulford who gave the congregation its name. "We go to Saratoga Springs in summer for health and recreation," she observed, "and we attend Bethesda Church there. Now, we are coming here to Florida in winter for health and recreation. Let us name this church 'Bethesda-by-the-Sea,' which means 'The House of Healing-by-the-Sea.' "

One of the first contributors to the first church building was Capt. E. N. Dimmich, from a first family in Palm Beach and first Mayor of the city. The first church of Bethesda was indeed the first Protestant church in southeast Florida, and it cost a fabulous $600.

Developer Henry Flagler brought his railroad here in 1892-93, and the community began to grow. By the spring of 1895, a new edifice was erected. This picturesque building served until the present church was dedicated in 1927, which was the dream of Canon James Townsend Russel who envisioned the beauty of a Spanish Gothic church placed amid trees and flowers.

An art historian said that Gothic architecture is the one clearest flame of the Christian spirit. It symbolizes the nobility and aspiration of the soul, the mystery of Christian worship, the sense of eminence of the Divine."

A BOOM-TIME LANDMARK

PALM BEACH—One of the great landmarks of Florida's flamboyant real estate boom is the handsome Palm Beach Biltmore Hotel here in the social center of America.

It hasn't always been known as the Biltmore. It acquired that name sometime after the namesake of the original hotel failed to show up for the opening celebration. Built in 1925 as the Alba Hotel, the structure was supposed to be named in honor of a Spanish noble- the Duke of Alba.

The elegant hotel is fit for a king or a duke or a socialite. The sprawling structure contains 543 rooms, and when it was opened in 1927, it was reported to have cost $7 million.

Since then, the Biltmore has gone through successive receiverships. It was used by the U. S. Coast Guard in 1943 and 1944 as a SPAR training base, and served the U. S. Navy as a hospital in 1945.

In 1962, the Biltmore was purchased by the R. H. Weissberg Corporation at a reported price of $4.3 million. When the corporation declared bankruptcy in December 1967, Lord Baltimore, Inc. took over operation of the hotel under a trusteeship of the federal court in Chicago. The hotel figured in further court actions in 1970.

In its hey-day, the Biltmore rated with Henry Flagler's The Breakers and other great hotels on the Gold Coast.

There is a rumor on the island of Palm Beach that, if money grew on trees, nobody would bother to pick it up. Exaggerated as that may be, there is no dispute that the town is America's most fabled home of millionaires.

DON MANUEL GONZALEZ

PENSACOLA—When the fiery Andrew Jackson arrived in Pensacola to take over Florida for the United States in 1821, he bumped into Don Manuel Gonzalez, a former Spanish soldier, Indian agent, and rancher. Not many people defied Jackson, but Gonzalez did.

The future President demanded that Gonzalez allow his son to guide Jackson to Fort Barrancas. Gonzalez snapped: "I would rather run a sword through his bosom than see him betray his Spanish King!" After that, Jackson and Gonzalez became fast friends.

Descendants of Manuel Gonzalez still live in Pensacola. The pretty frame home shown here was built in 1880 of virgin yellow pine by Manuel Francis Gonzalez, a Confederate veteran and the grandson of Jackson's friend. It is a Creole high-house with an apron roof, a design brought to the Gulf Coast from the French West Indies. The house is presently occupied by Gonzalez' son, Dickson, whose own son and grandson live next door. The latter is the sixth generation in America since the patriarch of the family was sent to New Orleans as a member of the Spanish Army in 1782.

The house is located at "Bohemia," on Escambia Bay, where the builder's great-grandmother, Marianna Bonifay, operated a brick kiln with slave labor from 1807 to 1832. The site is on U. S. 90, called Scenic Highway, on the northwest limits of Pensacola.

Manuel Francis Gonzalez was also a Pensacola merchant and newspaper publisher. The Gonzalez family is one of a number of Spanish colonial families whose descendants still live here.

THE HONEYMOON NEST

PENSACOLA—Don Francisco Moreno was a prolific patriarch of Pensacola whose life stretched from the days of George Washington to Reconstruction—from 1792 to 1882. He had three wives—his last was 16-year-old Mentoria Gonzalez; 27 children; and 127 grandchildren.

One Moreno daughter who had a front seat to history was Angela, the wife of the Secretary of the Navy of the Confederacy, Stephen Russell Mallory. Four of the Moreno sons gave their lives for the cause of the South in the Civil War.

Another daughter of whom Don Francisco was especially fond was Pearl (LaPerla). When she got married to Octavius H. Smith in 1879, her father presented the newlyweds with an attractive honeymoon cottage. The small Moreno cottage has been restored and today stands at 221 East Zaragoza Street, just off famed Seville Square.

The little love nest contained only two rooms and en enclosed back porch. The young people apparently needed no kitchen or dining room, since they ate with the Moreno family in the big house next door. The Smiths had one child born in the cottage. Later, another Moreno daughter, Corinne Fennel, owned and lived in the honeymoon haven. Recently, the Moreno cottage was the office of an advertising agency, Dodson. Craddock & Born Advertising Inc., whose president, Pat Dodson, is a leader in Pensacola's widespread historical preservation program.

The Moreno cottage stands on ground which has yielded innumerable artifacts from the early Spanish occupancy, dating to 1752.

PENSACOLA'S MOST HISTORIC HOUSE

PENSACOLA—Some call it the "Widow Troulett House," others refer to it as the "Charles LaValle House." But the scholars maintain that this is "without doubt the most original historic structure left, and may be the oldest surviving house in Pensacola."

And so in 1969, the Historic Pensacola Preservation Board rescued the ancient building which originally stood at 111 West Government Street, next to the Hispanic Museum, and then restored it for exhibition. This is in Pensacola's exciting Historic District at Seville Square.

The plot on which this very interesting and original house stood was part of a grant made by Gov. George Johnstown to Robert Ross Wadell of December 8, 1766, who sold the property the next year to James Thompson, a Pensacola merchant and member of one of the most important families in colonial America. The origin of this house is as yet unknwon. Its architecture is that of the eighteenth century, but its exact construction date is not available.

Earle W. Newton, former director of the Historic Pensacola Preservation Board (and former director of the Historic St. Augustine Preservation Board) said that the "Widow Troulett House" is the most original example of the typical French Creole cottage we have discovered.

The structure is remarkable for the early and unchanged character of its interior, Newton reported. In its four rooms, the only replacement seems to be the wood floor in the southwest room. Its wood frame contains brick nogging in all walls, even interior portions, to which plaster was applied directly.

PENSACOLA'S "NEW" CHRIST CHURCH

PENSACOLA—They call that interesting gray stucco structure with a red tile roof at the northwest corner of North Palafox and West Wright streets the "new" Christ Church. That becomes more of a misnomer every day, for the Episcopal sanctuary was built in 1902.

Age, of course, is relative. What makes this building "new" is that it became the new home of Christ Church when the parish moved from Old Christ Church in Pensacola's historic Seville Square.

Old Christ Church was erected in 1832, is still standing, and is believed to be one of the oldest Protestant churches in the state of Florida. It was built as the result of a movement that was started by Rachel Jackson, the devout and beautiful wife of Andrew Jackson, Florida's first Governor and later President of the United States. When the Jacksons came to Pensacola in 1821 to take over from the Spanish government, Rachel was appalled at the wickedness of the city and the lack of religious influence.

The lovely church served well for many decades, but in 1902 the "new" building was constructed at a hilly site overlooking downtown Pensacola. The entrance to this building is between engaged Ionic columns that support a broken pediment. The facade rises to a bell gable topped with a concrete cross. There is a part of the old church in the new one. The beautiful stained-glass windows of the original building were moved to the new church.

After the parish moved, the old church was used by a black Episcopal congregation for several years. Then, in 1936, Old Christ Church was deeded to the City of Pensacola to be used as a public library or a museum. For twenty years, the Public Library made its home here, moving in 1957 to its modern and more spacious quarters at Gregory and Springs streets. In August 1960, the Pensacola Historical Museum was opened in this beautiful old building.

Meanwhile, the New Christ Church carries on the good work that was started by Rachel Jackson who had "prayed and prayed that a minister of the Gospel would come over and help the Lord" in Pensacola.

POST-BELLUM SOCIAL CENTER

PENSACOLA—The pretty cottage next-door to Old Christ Church, overlooking historic Seville Square, is known as the Dorr House. It is painted a pleasing yellow, called Seville saffron, with white trim, and was restored by the Pensacola Heritage Foundation, Inc., which has its headquarters there.

Right after the Civil War, Pensacola enjoyed a lumber boom, and the Dorr House is a splendid example of post-bellum homes. Built between 1868 and 1871 by a socialite couple, Eben Walker and Clara Barkley Dorr, it was the site of many gala parties.

The structure features high ceilings, riff pine floors, slate mantles, and Gibbs windows on the front, and reflects Victorian architectural traditions. The house is across from the site of a British guardhouse in Seville Square (constructed about 1765), the foundations of which were uncovered by the Pensacola Preservation Society in 1966.

In its later life, before restoration, the Dorr House declined and became a rooming house. The Heritage Foundation volunteers donated several thousand hours redecorating the Dorr House. It is furnished with antiques, and the decor resembles that of the early Victorian period.

The attractive building was the first structure restored at Seville Square and triggered the vast restoration program underway in this historic city.

DID CIVIL WAR SHOOTING BEGIN IN FLORIDA?

PENSACOLA BEACH—Some historians will tell you the first shots of the Civil War were fired here at Fort Pickens, quite some time before the flareup at Fort Sumter.

During the tense weeks between the time when Florida seceded from the Union on January 19, 1861, and full-fledged war began, considerable maneuvering was going on. A young lieutenant decided that it would be better for the United States to take over and hold Fort Pickens, since it commands the whole of Pensacola harbor, and there were not enough Federal troops to save the Navy Yard, Fort Barrancas, and other properties. The Confederates actually had a truce with the United States, stipulating that they would not attack Fort Pickens if the Union did not try to reinforce it. The South felt that Fort Pickens "is not worth one drop of blood to us. Bloodshed may be fatal to our cause." Later, the Union violated the truce since President Lincoln did not feel bound by pledges of the former administration. In the meantime, shots had been exchanged.

Fort Pickens was built in 1834 on orders from President Adams. It was constructed under supervision of Capt. William H. Chase, an army engineer who later, as a Confederate general, was ordered to capture the fort, but failed. The Battel of Santa Rosa Island was fought here in October; the Confederates lost, and later abandoned the entire Pensacola area.

Fort Pickens became a military prison. One of the most famous prisoners was Geronimo, the Apache Indian marauder, who was kept here from 1886 until 1888. He was so fierce-looking, Pensacola parents disciplined unruly children by threatening to put them in a cell with Geronimo.

GRACIOUS LIVING IN THE 1800s

POINT WASHINGTON—Heading along U. S. 98 between Panama City and Pensacola, don't go too fast or you'll miss the turn-off for "Eden," a lovely home that depicts Southern living in the late 1800s. Watch for State Road 395. Eden is on that road, just a mile off U. S. 98, and is now a state park.

The handsome frame house, sheltered by moss-draped oaks, was restored to its original glamor by Miss Lois Maxon after she bought it in 1963. The white-columned mansion was built before the turn of the century by a lumber baron who had his millhands construct the home of heart pine and cypress.

The Eden estate is at the southeast corner of Choctawhatchee Bay. The virgin timber was floated down the river to the mill for processing, then taken to Pensacola for finishing. Through the years, Eden was a social center in the panhandle, but was finally abandoned. Vandalism and decay were wrecking the place when Miss Maxon saved and restored it.

The recent owner set about to furnish the handsome mansion with a priceless collection of art and antiques, including many pieces from Europe, and others from family heirlooms dating back to the 1600s. There are such attractions as altar candlesticks from Italy, Adams knife urns from Scotland, a French grandfather clock 200 years old, a seventeenth-century cherry bed and French fruitwood chest, and many other elegant objects.

Eden, open to visitors for a nominal admission fee, contains eleven acres of land with some of the trees three hundred years old.

CITY GATE GUARDS ST. AUGUSTINE

ST. AUGUSTINE—There it stands today, just as it has for more than a century and a half, the bulky but attractive city gate that "guards" St. Augustine.

Way back when it was built in 1808, the city gate was an integral part of the Cubo line. This was the defense the Spanish constructed in 1704, and which stretched from the historic Castillo de San Marcos across town to the Sebastian River. It made the oldest city secure from invasion by land.

The impressive coquina pylons replaced a wooden house which had guarded the gateway since 1738. At one time, a two-leaf gate stood between the stone pillars, and a bridge spanned the moat in front of the Cubo line.

No longer used to repel visitors but to welcome them, the city gate leads into narrow St. George Street (Calle Real), the only street to run the entire length of St. Augustine.

The Cubo line figures prominently in the current restoration program underway here. At one time, the defense was a parapet formed by palm logs. The Spanish got busy and built strong earthworks across the peninsula after the British had invaded St. Augustine during Queen Anne's War in 1702. South Carolina's Governor James Moore and 500 men seized St. Augustine and besieged the fort unsuccessfully for 50 days. As a farewell gift, Moore set fire to the town, destroyed the Spanish missions, and carried off 1,400 Indians as slaves.

NOT THE "OLDEST HOUSE"

ST. AUGUSTINE—There's plenty of authentic history to the quaint little house at 14 St. Francis Street, even though it doesn't meet the original claims of being the "Oldest House in the United States."

There have been houses standing on this site since the 1600s, but the present building was erected around 1727—which is plenty old! When British troops swept into St. Augustine in 1702, they didn't leave a single house standing.

When this town began to attract tourists in sizeable numbers, the house was billed as the oldest in the nation. The *Saturday Evening Post,* aware of the old houses in New England that date back to the seventeenth century, challenged the claim. The house promoter sued the magazine and won because the *Post* could not disprove the claim, even though the promoter could not prove the correctness of his claim either.

Later, the St. Augustine Historical Society acquired the property and thoroughly investigated the antiquity of the rugged house. It is now promoted simply as the oldest house in the oldest city. Tomas Gonzalez y Hernandez was the first occupant in the early 1700s.

The first-floor walls are constructed from the natural shellstone called coquina, quarried on nearby Anastasia Island. The floor is of tabby, a mixture of lime, sand, and shell.

There is much about the home that reflects life in the Spanish colony during the eighteenth century. The Historical Society maintains an outstanding museum and an excellent library in the building.

OLD
SPANISH TRAIL
ZERO MILESTONE
S. AUGUSTINE FLA.
TO
SAN DIEGO CALIF.

THE OLD SPANISH TRAIL

ST. AUGUSTINE—Eventually, Interstate 10 will speed motorists cross-country from the East coast of Florida to the West coast of California. Needless to say, it will be a far cry from the earliest of transcontinental highways which began here in St. Augustine.

The beginning of that road was the Old Spanish Trail, which really was a pathway cut through jungle-like underbrush and swamps by persevering priests during the first Spanish colonial period (1565 to 1763) as they went about establishing missions in the interior. Aside from the clergy, the Spanish did little about roads because the early *conquistadores* believed the state was an island, and they searched for water routes to connect the villages.

Near downtown St. Augustine is an unusual marker which is designated the "Zero Milestone" of the Old Spanish Trail, the first throughway in the new world which creeped cross-country until it reached San Diego. The unique landmark is a sphere made from native coquina rock quarried here. It is sizable, six foot in diameter, and was erected in 1928 by the local Exchange Club.

Traveling on the Trail was risky business because Indians frequently attacked the strangers. And when the English in Georgia coveted Florida, raiders often slipped across the border to harass the trailblazers. As time passed, the trail became used more and more. Gen. Andrew Jackson, later to become Florida's first governor, marched along the trail when he entered Florida during the First Seminole War. In 1824, a Federal highway was authorized between St. Augustine and Pensacola which generally followed the Trail.

THE GREAT FREEZE CAUSED CHURCH TO MOVE

ST. CLOUD—The little church with the tall spire that is now a landmark in St. Cloud once stood in the nearby community of Narcoossee. But the Great Freeze of 1895 virtually wiped out that town, and the Episcopal sanctuary was moved.

Narcoossee was "essentially an English colony where English customs prevail and prayers for the Queen and Royal Family are said," according to Pennington in his "Episcopal Church in Florida." The freeze made the village a ghost town.

St. Luke's Church had one of the highest wooden spires in the state—72 feet high—and resembled Holy Cross Church in Sanford. First services were held in 1884, although the building wasn't finished until 1898. It was consecrated by the Right Reverend William Crane, D.D., bishop of the Missionary District of South Florida.

The English people reportedly brought many of the carvings and ornate decorations for the church interior with them from their mother country. Proud of its Gothic architecture, the church has long been noted for its purity and beauty.

In 1930, it was decided to transfer the building from Narcoossee to St. Cloud, where another church, St. Peter's, was going. The structure was dismantled piece by piece, and each piece marked so that the church could be reassembled in its original form.

It was rededicated on Easter Day 1931. Out of deference to the first occupants, the congregation at St. Cloud renamed their building the Church of St. Luke and St. Peter.

FLORIDA'S LARGEST PUBLIC WORKS PROJECT

ST. PETERSBURG—Once upon a time, a rickety old ferry plodded between St. Petersburg and Palmetto. Years of discussion about the need for a bridge between the two points finally brought action, and in 1954 a giant span was opened and dedicated.

The Sunshine Skyway is the largest public works project ever built by the State of Florida. The original two-lane structure has since gotten a twin as two more lanes were added that opened in 1969.

Talk of a bridge between Pinellas and Manatee goes back to 1912. The first actual link between the areas came with the start of the Bee Line Ferry in 1924. A $7-million high-level bridge was approved by the government in 1925, but area-wide political squabbles stalled it. Finally, during the administration of Gov. Fuller Warren, the Sunshine Skyway—an ultra-modern, high-level bridge so high that ocean-going vessels can pass underneath it—was started.

The first structure cost $22 million, and the additional two lanes of a parallel bridge about $25 million. The bridge is over four miles long and rises 250 feet or 15 stories high above water. The central span rises on a five-percent grade from trestle approaches 21 feet above water. The causeway offers ten miles of beach recreational facilities, and there are catwalks for fishing on four small bridges in the system.

HMS BOUNTY REPLICA RESTS IN PEACE

ST. PETERSBURG—The original *HMS Bounty* had a stormy and infamous career. But a replica of the historic vessel rests peacefully amid a Tahitian setting at the Vinoy Park Basin here and basks in the compliments tourists pay her.

Bounty II was reconstructed from original drawings in the files of the British Admiralty by Metro-Goldwyn-Mayer movie studio. After starring in the epic, "Mutiny on the *Bounty*," the ship was brought here for permanent exhibit after a 60,000-mile journey to the South Seas for filming and promotional cruises.

The original *Bounty* had been a coastal trader named *Bethia.* The Navy of King George III selected her for Lt. William Bligh's mission to the South Seas in 1789, where she was to collect young transplants of the breadfruit tree and carry them to Jamaica for cultivation as cheap food for slaves.

Bounty II, built in Nova Scotia, is a 480-ton vessel, 114 feet long, and carries 10,000 square feet of canvas. Below, all quarters are decorated in detail with eighteenth-century furniture, fittings, and priceless antiques. A replica of the *Bounty's* original anchor is also aboard, as is a replica of the longboat in which Captain Bligh was put to sea during the mutiny by Fletcher Christian.

This exhibit of maritime history features recordings of the voices of Clark Gable and Charles Laughton as they speak the words of Christian and Bligh that led to the best-known mutiny in history.

MIZNER ON THE WEST COAST

ST. PETERSBURG—The legendary Addison Mizner, whose press agent billed him as "The Poet of Architects," was the most noted designer along Florida's glittering lower East coast. But his influence also extended to Jacksonville at the northeast corner of the state, and to St. Petersburg on the West coast.

Mizner, who with his brother Wilson became known as the "Legendary Mizners," designed the Cloister Inn at Boca Raton, the Everglades Club, and numerous homes for the wealthy in posh Palm Beach. Among his multimillionaire clients were Joseph P. Kennedy, the Vanderbilts, the Wanamakers, and the Stotesburys.

Addison rode high, wide, and handsome throughout the boisterous boom in Florida real estate in the 1920s. But the grandiose activity collapsed, and Mizner's bubble also burst. He continued to design buildings wherever he could. He was the architect for the Riverside Baptist Church in Jacksonville, and then he came over to St. Petersburg. He was working on the "Williams home" at 510 Park Street, North (shown in photo), when he died in 1933. The home is a beautiful showplace to this day and features the deft touch of the famed architect. The house is noted for its two-story rotunda which centers the house. It was reputed to have cost $500,000 in the 1930s.

Considered one of Florida's finest mansions, the Park Street home was sold to Charles Holin, owner of Holin Tackle Co. of Detroit and Windsor, Ontario, in 1967.

A CIRCUS KING'S LEGACY

SARASOTA—They all laughed when John Ringling revealed in 1925 that he was going to establish a great art museum on the grounds of his magnificent $1,500,000 residence here.

This man was a gaudy showman, not a refined lover of art, his scoffers noted. Ringling was not an art collector, and he really knew very little about it.

But the mighty circus king learned about art quickly, and set about acquiring the country's largest and finest collection of paintings of the sixteenth, seventeenth, and eighteenth centuries. Ringling liked them because of their vitality. He started building a museum to house them, but the Great Depression hit and John Ringling ran into financial difficulties, at least as far as ready cash was concerned. He never lost sight of his goal, though, and the great museum finally opened in 1930.

The building itself is a sight to behold. It is styled after a fifteenth-century Florentine villa and is said to be the most beautiful example of Italian Renaissance architecture in the United States. A tremendous bronze cast of Michelangelo's statue of David dominates the Italian garden court.

Ringling died in 1936 and left his art museum and its collections, valued at $15 million, and many other properties, to the State of Florida. A court fight ensued. Ringling's second wife, whom he had divorced, sought a settlement. After years of litigation, Florida got museum. The second Mrs. Ringling received one dollar.

SARASOTA'S ASOLO THEATRE

SARASOTA—Some people say Sarasota is "culture-happy," and the town won't argue about that. One of the daintiest and most delightful contributions to this culture is the gem-like Asolo Theatre which adorns the grounds of the estate of circus king John Ringling.

The Asolo is the only original eighteenth-century Italian theatre in America. It was built in 1798 in the old castle of Catherine Cornaro in the hill town of Asolo, near Venice. The small, round auditorium spotlighted some of the most brilliant actors of its time during a period of more than a century at Asolo. Vacationers to the Venice playground packed the tiny theatre, among them Robert Browning who came again and again.

One of the greats who performed at Asolo was the lovely Italian actress Eleonora Duse. Her role in the history of the theatre was recalled during a visit to the Ringling Museum and theatre in 1959 by Miss Katherine Cornell. She said Miss Duse was her inspiration and, standing where Duse had performed in her own youth, she felt "the continuing life of a tradition."

The State of Florida, which owns and operates the Ringling Museum, bought the Asolo Theatre in 1950 from an antiquarian in Venice and had it shipped to Sarasota. The theatre had been dismantled in 1930 to make way for a modern movie house and remained in storage until the director of the Ringling Museum recommended its purchase to the Florida State Legislature.

OSCEOLA'S ENEMIES ACKNOWLEDGED HIS VIRTUES

SILVER SPRINGS—An angry young man of his times was the hand-some and virile Indian warrior, Osceola. A native of Hamilton County, Osceola moved to the Ocala area where he grew up and where he achieved fame in the Indian war to prevent shipment of the Seminole tribe to Oklahoma by the U. S. Government.

There's a bronze-painted statue on the edge of sparkling Silver Springs that depicts Osceola in his most famous pose. It shows the irate young sub-chief displaying his emotions by stabbing a treaty which allegedly had been signed with the whites by fellow tribesmen. "The only treaty I will execute is with this," growled Osceola, slash-ing the piece of paper with a big knife. "This is my mark, I will make no other." His inflammatory oration at Silver Springs on that memo-rable day, October 23, 1834, fired up his race and ignited the Seven Years' War.

As a strapping youth wise to the world of "Ocali country," Osce-ola served as a guide and scout to Territorial Governor William P. DuVal. Later he was friendly with the Indian agent, Gen. Wiley Thompson. This friendship ended when Thompson ordered the cap-ture of the chief's lovely wife, Morning Dew, because she was sup-posed to be the daughter of a runaway slave. The mighty chief swore vengeance. He became an important military genius and a noted strat-egist in American history. Even his enemies lauded him as a "patriot and warrior." He was treacherously captured under a flag of truce and imprisoned in St. Augustine.

THE SKEETERS GOBBLED UP THE BATS!

SUGAR LOAF SHORES—Through scientific mosquito control, man finally has conquered his most vicious opponent here on this idyllic spot in the Florida Keys, not too far away from Key West. A picturesque tropical community has developed where once the pesky mosquito made life unbearable for human beings.

A continuing reminder of those bygone days provides a unique historic landmark. It's an odd-shaped structure built many years ago as a motel for bats who were invited to come to Sugar Loaf Key to feast on all those fat mosquitoes. But, alas, as soon as the bats were let out of their fine home, they disappeared. An improbable legend has it that the skeeters themselves gobbled up the thousand imported bats.

Sugar Loaf Key, which gets its name from an Indian midden resembling an old-fashioned sugar loaf, has a colorful history dating back to about 1910. At that time, Miami Beach had less than six hundred residents, and Key West was a flourishing city with some twenty-five thousand souls. A man named C. W. Chase came here and started a sponge farm. Other spongers swiped his crop, and he sold his property to Richter C. Perky, a financier from Kansas City, Missouri.

The native mosquitoes didn't like human company, except as a banquet table. And Perky was their kind of meat. A writer who visited the tiny isle reported that the mosquitoes "possessed a sixth sense when it came to anticipating the imminent approach of tender northern human pelts upon which to quench their sanguine thirst."

Perky went ahead and built a large restaurant, a gambling casino, cottages—and two bat towers! Those towers were the idea of a visitor from New Jersey, a professor who sold Perky on the idea that the bats could board in them and devour the pests.

The tall 50-foot tower, of obelisk shape, offered a quaint conversation piece for those coming this way. Bats were imported from Cuba, but two batches of them escaped, and Perky gave up his experiment. The remaining tower stands just off U. S. 1, the lifeline-highway through the Florida Keys.

THE CAPITOL IS AS OLD AS THE STATE ITSELF

TALLAHASSEE—For more than a century and a half, many Florida towns have coveted the State capital, but this hilly community named "old town" by the Seminoles proudly continues as seat of government. The core of the State Capitol building itself dates back to the very beginning of statehood and, though sagging and dilapidated, continues to house executive and legislative departments.

Tallahassee was selected as the site for the capital in 1823, primarily because it was midway between the two populated cities of Florida, Pensacola and St. Augustine. The first Capitol building was a log cabin near the site of the present structure.

A two-story "modern" Capitol was begun in 1826. The present permanent building was started in 1829 and featured front and rear entrances through porticos each having six Doric columns 13 feet in diameter and 34 feet in height. This structure, the core of today's building, was finally completed in 1834—the year Florida became a state.

As early as 1824, a petition from "sundry inhabitants" of Gadsden County prayed for the removal of the capital to a site on some navigable water. These efforts for removal have continued off and on since then, and as late as 1967 Orlando made a strong bid to become the state capital. But Tallahassee's "hopsitality" has always won, as noted by poet Sidney Lanier, after a referendum in 1901 gave the city the nod over Jacksonville, Ocala, and St. Augustine.

Tallahassee is the only Southern capital that did not fall into the hands of Union troops during the Civil War.

"KNOTT HOUSE"

TALLAHASSEE—One of Florida's oldest and most attractive houses stands majestically in downtown Tallahassee today just as it has since it was built in 1831. It is known as the "Knott House," belonging to the family of the late W. V. Knott, a long-time political figure who acquired the structure during the 1920s.

The state was just a young, struggling territory, and Tallahassee then as now its capital, when the frame home at East Park Avenue and Calhoun Street was built. It was a wedding gift that Thomas Holmes Hagner, former United States Minister to the Court of Saint James in London, presented to his bride, the former Katherine Gamble of Virginia. Its origin was reported in a booklet issued by the Tallahassee Rotary Club. It noted that Mrs. Hagner brought the first japonica plants to Florida. They had been brought, as a gift for her mother, by General Marcer from the court of King George.

The house had been enlarged by 1848. It had a number of owners before Knott acquired it. Knott removed the one-story front porch and replaced it with a two-story portice and columns. The house faces Lewis Park, where the famous May Oak stands, the giant tree that has provided an umbrella for colorful May Day festivities for nearly a century and a half. Another landmark is situated across from the Knott House: the old Cherokee Hotel, favorite lodging for Florida politicians, which was torn down later.

Knott was State Treasurer and State Comptroller, and narrowly missed becoming Governor in a hotly contested race in 1916.

OLD SLAVE QUARTERS ARE
SURROUNDED BY MODERN TALLAHASSEE

TALLAHASSEE–Truly a distinctive landmark, hidden away behind another historic structure, The Columns, in the maze of modern Tallahassee, is the Old Slave Quarters.

They go together, the lovely mansion of the early territorial days and the accompanying slave quarters which served both as living quarters for the servants and as an area for preparing bountiful meals for the "big house." Both buildings formerly were at 105 West Park Street at Adams on property owned by the First Baptist Church, but were removed in 1971. The Columns was moved to Park and Duval streets and became the headquarters of the Tallahassee Chamber of Commerce.

It is doubtful there are other typical slave cabins like this one left anywhere else in Florida. This, even though the vast Tallahassee area originally thrived on great cotton farms, an activity which in those days depended entirely on slave labor.

The Columns, and probably the slave cottage behind it, was built by Benjamin Chaires who came to pioneer Florida in the territorial days. When completed in 1835, it was the largest and perhaps swankiest house in the capital. The house and the neighboring First Presbyterian Church were sometimes used as a refuge against marauding Indians.

Chaires was a leading figure in Florida's first financial institution, the Union Bank. Also involved in the bank, and a purchaser of The Columns, was a millionaire, William Williams, nicknamed "Money" Williams because he supposedly arrived with a wagonload of money to start the bank.

"THE TALLAHASSEE GIRL"

TALLAHASSEE—To most everyone at the time, Gen. Richard Keith Cass was a man to be admired, even idolized. But to the mother of his bride-to-be, the adventuresome gentleman was "only an Indian fighter" and not worthy of the hand of her aristocratic daughter.

It wasn't Call so much who brought contempt from Mary Kirkman's mother, it was his best friend, Gen. Andrew Jackson. When the future President tried to intercede for his aide, Mrs. Kirkman pulled a shotgun on him and chased him away—a feat not accomplished by anyone else. This happened in Nashville.

Finally, Call and his sweetheart eloped. The "Indian fighter" was determined to build as fine a home in pioneer Florida as his beloved had left in Nashville. So it was that in 1825 he built "The Grove" in Tallahassee. It was constructed in a typical neo-classical design, and some ideas were adapted from Jackson's beautiful mansion, "The Hermitage," near Nashville.

Call became territorial governor of Florida, and it was at "The Grove" that their daughter, Ellen Call Long, grew up, the first white child born in Tallahassee. "The Grove" was the setting for Maurice Thompson's novel *The Tallahassee Girl.*

The elegant estate (which has a family cemetery in the rear) has remained in the Call family, and is now owned by former Gov. and Mrs. LeRoy Collins (she was Mary Call before her marriage). The Collinses lived at "The Grove" much of the time he was Governor, because the State was building a new executive mansion across the street at the time.

HERE LIES

W^m. ASHLEY and NANCY ASHLEY,

MASTER, AND SERVANT,

Faithful to each other in that relation
in life, in death they are not separated.

Stranger consider and be wiser;
In the Grave all human distinction,
of race, or caste, mingle together
in one common dust.

*To commemorate their fidelity to each other
this stone was erected by their Executor
JOHN JACKSON,
1873.*

"STRANGER CONSIDER AND BE WISER"

TAMPA—A prominent Tampan in the mid-1800s was William Ashley, who had moved here from Virginia in 1837, and clerked for the Army sutler. His home was located on the southeast corner of Lafayette Street (now J. F. Kennedy Boulevard) and Water Street, in what is now downtown Tampa.

When Tampa was incorporated as a city in late 1855, Ashley was elected City Clerk. One recognition given this leading citizen was the naming of Ashley Street.

Historian Karl H. Grismer relates in his story on Tampa about Ashley dying in 1873 and being buried in Oak Lawn Cemetery.

"Shortly afterward a Negro woman died who had long been Ashley's servant," Grismer reported. "The relationship which had existed between Ashley and Nancy was much closer than that which normally existed between master and servant but, strange to say, it was not frowned upon by the community."

The history states that upon Nancy's death she was buried in the same grave. Ashley's executor, John Jackson, had a tombstone erected "to commemorate their fidelity to each other." The inscription on the gravestone reads:

"Here Lies Wm Ashley and Nancy Ashley, Master, and Servant. Faithful to each other in that relation in life, in death they are not seperated (sic). *Stranger consider and be wiser, In the Grave all human distinction of race or caste mingle together in one common dust."*

ROMAN CATHOLICISM IN TAMPA

TAMPA—Roman Catholicism is the oldest religion in the Tampa Bay area, dating back to the visits by the Spanish Conquistadores in the early sixteenth century. At least five Franciscans were with Panfilo de Narvaez when he touched down in this section in 1528. Hernando de Soto also had priests in his party when he landed in 1539 on the gulf coast (presumably near Bradenton), and then moved northward in the vicinity of present-day Tampa.

This bit of church history was noted by Adiel J. Moncrief, church editor of the *Tampa Tribune,* when he wrote a story marking the 100th anniversary of the founding of the Sacred Heart Church in 1960. Originally called St. Louis Church, the parishioners met in a small frame building on the present site of the magnificent Sacred Heart Church on Florida Avenue in downtown Tampa. The early mission established here ceased to exist in 1572, and for 250 years there were no Roman Catholic services.

In 1853, County Commissioners set aside land for use by Catholics. Mass had been said in different places for the lack of a church, as for instance in the home of Mayor J. John Jackson.

The county land gift was exchanged for the present site, and the beautiful church built. The parish started a school for boys, known as Sacred Heart College. It is now called Jesuit High School.

THE OLD WATER TOWER

TAMPA—Motorists arriving in Tampa on Interstate 75 or two other arteries, Nebraska Avenue or Florida Avenue, are greeted by the imposing sight of an old water tower as they cross Hillsborough River at the north end of town.

This is a landmark from the Florida boom days. Old-timers in the Sulphur Springs community say the stairs inside are a little creaky and old, but the structure itself is as sound and solid as the day it was built back in the 1920s.

Shooting 225 feet in the air, the tower still operates. Clear artesian water is pumped from the spring beneath its base to the top of the tower where it is stored in a 125,000-gallon tank, and distributed to a number of businesses in the vicinity.

Joe Cy Richardson, a developer, built the tower in 1927. The story goes that it was divided at certain levels into seven rooms, and that it was planned to use these as facilities for the entertainment of winter visitors. But it has served only as a water tower.

There is a four-foot platform at the top, and those who have had the opportunity to scan the horizon from this vantage point say it offers a fascinating view for miles around.

From time to time, civic leaders urge use of the old landmark for some sort of tourist attraction, possibly as a picnic park and scenic lookout tower. But the city fathers and the owners of the property have never gotten together.

THE *JOSE GASPARILLA*

TAMPA—Through two world wars, the Tampa Shipyard turned out fighting ships, many of them earning fame in sea battles. But the most unique vessel built by the yard, and itself quite famous, was not a real warship—it was the *Jose Gasparilla,* flagship of Tampa's gay "Ye Mystic Krewe of Gasparilla."

The only ship in the world built in modern times solely for piratical purposes, this is also the world's most photographed ship. A replica of a West Indiaman, vintage 1800, the Krewe vessel is used once a year in February to transport the play-like pirates as they "invade" Tampa and cap off the exciting event with a triumphal parade through downtown streets and thence to the Florida State Fair grounds.

More than 700,000 people pack the streets and every vantage point to watch the frolicking pirates "take" the community. Nearly every onlooker has a camera and keeps clicking away from every angle possible. Many thousands of other people watch the spectacle on television.

The *Jose Gasparilla* was built by the Tampa Shipyard during 1953 and 1954 and was commissioned on January 5, 1954. She has a displacement of 300 tons. The overall length is 164 feet and six inches, and she has a 35-foot beam. Three masts tower some one hundred feet skyward. During the invasion, pirates perch precariously high in the rigging and scare the crowds with their daredevilry. The all-steel ship has cannon at all ports, and they actually fire salutes. More than three hundred flags and pennants of every color flutter in the breeze. During Invasion Week, the ship is moored at the University of Tampa docks, and visitors are welcome aboard. This ship replaced an old wooden ship that was condemned by the Coast Guard.

CENTER OF GREEK COMMUNITY LIFE

TARPON SPRINGS—As Florida churches go, St. Nicholas Greek Orthodox Church in the heart of Tarpon Springs is not "old." But it is literally in the hearts of all who live here. As one observer points out, St. Nicholas is the very center, the mortar of Greek community life.

The sponge industry developed here at the turn of the century and professional divers were imported from Greece. By 1903, the town began celebrating Epiphany Day in January, one of the most holy days of the Greek Orthodox Church. In the same year, the first St. Nicholas Church was started. It was finished in 1907, a small edifice seating only 250 people and costing $15,000.

This small church was much in contrast to today's gorgeous and elegant cathedral which was dedicated in 1941. The beautiful Byzantine structure has a glistening interior of white Grecian marble which serves to highlight the magnificent beauty of stained-glass windows and icons, offset by several huge, delicate crystal chandeliers. There is a white Carrara-marble altar dedicated to the memory of the Rev. Theophilos Karaphillis who served the church as pastor from 1922 until his death in 1963.

Thousands throng to Tarpon Springs each January 6 to watch a church dignitary toss a golden cross into the icy cold waters of Spring Bayou and to watch the excitement as many young Greek lads dive in to retrieve it. The "winner" is assured of good luck all year.

THE "LITTLE GOVERNOR" FROM ARIZONA

TARPON SPRINGS—The large two-story frame house with wide verandahs at both levels is a landmark here. It's the original home of Anson Peacely-Killen Safford (usually written "A. P. K." Safford), the founder of this community.

Safford came here after exciting careers in the East and out West. This area was part of the huge 4-million acre "Disston land sale." The Internal Improvement Fund, headed by Gov. William D. Bloxham, sold the vast holdings to the saw manufacturer at 25 cents an acre. Safford came to Florida to help the Disston syndicate develop the holdings, and he founded Tarpon Springs in 1882.

A native of Vermont, Safford at the age of 20 made the hard cross-country trek to California. He was a gold miner and served in the California legislature. Later he drifted to Nevada where he was elected Recorder in a county there. He was also Surveyor General for the state. His political connections got him appointment as territorial governor of Arizona by President Grant in 1869. He became known as the "Little Governor," fought the Apache Indians, and started the public school system in that state. Safford, Arizona, is named for him.

The 1873 Arizona legislature handed Governor Safford a divorce through a law which passed with but one dissenting vote. The Governor himself signed it into law. He married again in 1877.

In Tarpon Springs, Safford was a real leader and one of the founders of the Universalist Church. He died in 1891 at the age of 61.

DOOLITTLE'S RAIDERS

VALPARAISO—On the first day of March 1942, the dashing, daring air-racer-turned-warrior called together a group of young airmen at nearby Eglin Field, and laid out in no uncertain terms what was ahead: "If you men have any idea that this isn't the most dangerous thing you've ever been on, don't even start this training period. You can drop out now."

Nobody dropped out. Everybody on this special task force turned to, and the next few weeks at this isolated northwest Florida base were frenzied. Jimmy Doolittle was training crews to take off in B25 land bombers from an aircraft carrier to bomb Japan!

Families lived here and at Fort Walton, but rarely saw their men. The fliers were practicing short takeoffs, night flying, and scooting through the skies from Eglin to Fort Myers, thence across the Gulf of Mexico at very low level to Houston and back home.

Precisely at 12:30 p.m. on April 18, America struck back at the Japanese. Doolittle and his Raiders were in action! They took off from the *USS Hornet,* sixteen planeloads of them, and invaded the Emperor's homeland. Tokyo, Yokohama, Nagoya, and Kobe were targets. The planes had been spotted, and took off earlier than planned. Most of them were forced to crash before reaching their intended destination in friendly China, but the strike was a morale booster at home.

Today, just inside the city limits of "Val-P," there is a memorial to this historic event. The last B-25 built is a central part of it.

YOUNG CADETS AND OLD MEN
SAVED THE CAPITAL

WOODVILLE—This tiny community on U. S. 319, about 15 miles south of Tallahassee, is the site of the famous Battle of Natural Bridge in which a brave band of college cadets joined a motley militia of old men and wounded veterans to save the capital from capture in the waning days of the Civil War.

A large flotilla of Union forces under Gen. John Newton had landed at St. Marks, planning to take the East River bridge, to destroy the railroad to Tallahassee, and to capture the State capital itself. The alarm was sounded. Young cadets from West Florida Seminary (now Florida State University) and old men of the town quickly formed a courageous fighting unit, led by Confederate Gen. Sam Jones.

The two forces clashed here, where the St. Marks River disappears underground, rising to the surface a short distance to the south. The Rebels had four cannons and poured the fire on the attackers, forcing them to retreat. Only three of the Rebels were killed that day; the Federals lost 148. The Southerners were outnumbered three to one.

Great was the celebration in Florida's capital city. Tallahassee was the only Confederate capital east of the Mississippi that never fell into Federal hands.

Today, Florida State University proudly displays the Confederate Battle Streamer, an honor won that day when the cadets bested the Union soldiers at Natural Bridge.

OTHER BOOKS BY HAMPTON DUNN

published by E. A. Seemann Publishing, Inc.
P. O. Box K, Miami, Florida 33156

YESTERDAY'S CLEARWATER

"You really don't have to be from Clearwater to enjoy the sweep of nostalgia that comes with the picture pages of steepled churches, the broad causeways, the moss-and-magnolia waterways." *Miami News*   *160 pp., cloth, $8.95*

YESTERDAY'S ST. PETERSBURG

"The serious student of Florida history is fortunate to have at his disposal a single volume that presents this much information in an accessible format." *Tampa Tribune-Times*   *160 pp., cloth, $7.95*

YESTERDAY'S TALLAHASSEE

". . . the best of the series on Florida cities. Dunn has pulled together a whole lot of old photographs and drawings going back to the early territorial days." *Tallahassee Democrat*   *144 pp., cloth, $7.95*

YESTERDAY'S TAMPA ®

"Another remarkable job of updating yesterday's Florida has been done. . . . an outstanding collection of photographs which highlights the West Coast city." *Miami Herald*   *160 pp., cloth, $7.95*